CON*T*

MW01048048

1 2 3 4 5 6 7 8 9 0

Psalm 27:4

Rick Klein

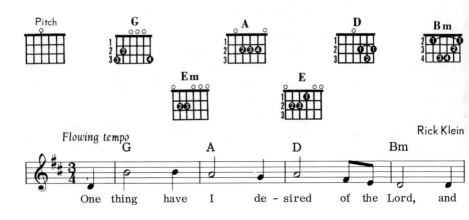

Flowing tempo

One thing have I de - sired of the Lord, and

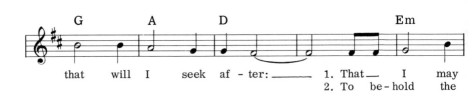

that will I seek af - ter: _____ 1. That ___ I may
2. To be - hold the

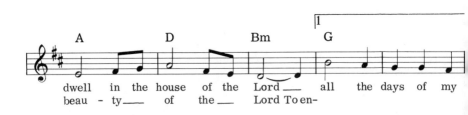

dwell in the house of the Lord ___ all the days of my
beau - ty ___ of the ___ Lord To en-

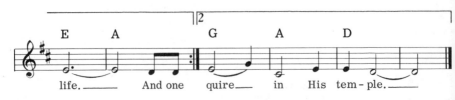

life. _____ And one quire ___ in His tem - ple. _____

I Have Decided to Follow Jesus

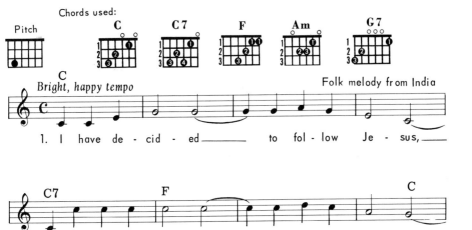

Chords used:

Pitch   C   C7   F   Am   G7

Bright, happy tempo   Folk melody from India

1. I have de - cid - ed ___ to fol - low Je - sus, ___

___ I have de - cid - ed ___ to fol - low Je - sus, ___

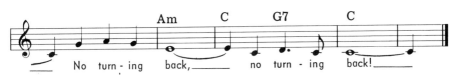

___ I have de - cid - ed ___ to fol - low Je - sus ___

No turn - ing back, ___ no turn - ing back! ___

2. The world behind me, the cross before me - No turning back, no turning back

3. Though no one join me, still I will follow - No turning back, no turning back.

4. Take the whole world but give me Jesus, - I'll follow Him, I'll follow Him.

He Is Lord

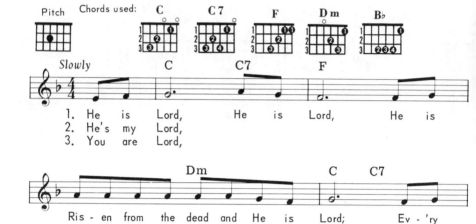

1. He is Lord, He is Lord, He is
2. He's my Lord,
3. You are Lord,

Ris - en from the dead and He is Lord; Ev - 'ry

knee shall bow, ev - 'ry tongue con - fess that

Je - sus Christ is Lord.

Jesus Is His Name

Chords used:

Bill Bay

Slowly, with feeling

1. Al - might - y God, Ev - er - last - ing Fa - ther,
   Light of the world, Rock of Sal - va - tion,
2. Bright, Morn - ing star, His Ho - ly one (the)
   Re - deem - er, Al - pha and O - me - ga,

Won - der - ful, Coun - se - lor, Prince of Peace.
Im - man - u - el, Bless - ed Lamb of God.
Res - ur - rec - tion and the Life, The Mes - si - ah.
The Word made flesh, Je - sus is His name.

Door of the sheep, Son of God, The
Ser - vant of God, Lord of Hosts, The

Way, Truth, and Life Je - sus is His name.
Bread of Life Je - sus is His name.

Blessed Assurance

2. Perfect submission, perfect delight,
    Visions of rapture now burst on my sight;
    Angels descending, bring from above
    Echoes of mercy, whispers of love. (to chorus)

3. Perfect submission, all is at rest,
    I, in my Savior, am happy and blest;
    Watching and waiting, looking above,
    Filled with His goodness, lost in His love. (to chorus)

Blessed be the Name

He Lives

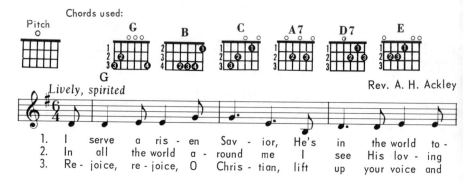

Chords used:

Pitch · G · B · C · A7 · D7 · E

G

Lively, spirited

Rev. A. H. Ackley

1. I serve a ris - en Sav - ior, He's in the world to -
2. In all the world a - round me I see His lov - ing
3. Re - joice, re - joice, O Chris - tian, lift up your voice and

B · C

day;____ I know that He is liv - ing, what-
care,____ And though my heart grows wear - y I
sing ____ E - ter - nal hal - le - lu - jahs To

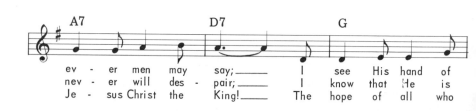

A7 · D7 · G

ev - er men may say;____ I see His hand of
nev - er will des - pair;____ I know that He is
Je - sus Christ the King!____ The hope of all who

mer - cy, I hear His voice of cheer,____ And
lead - ing, through all the storm - y blast ____ The
seek Him, the Help of all who find,____ None

just the time I need Him___ He's al - ways near.___
day of His ap - pear - ing ___ will come at last.___
oth - er is so lov - ing, ___ so good and kind.___

REFRAIN

He lives, ___ He lives, ___ Christ Je - sus lives_ to -

day! ___ He walks with me and talks with me a -

long life's nar___ row way.___ He lives,___ He

lives, ___ Sal - va - tion to im - part! ___ You

ask me how I know He lives? He lives with -in my heart.___

Come Taste the Beauty of the Lord

Rick Klein

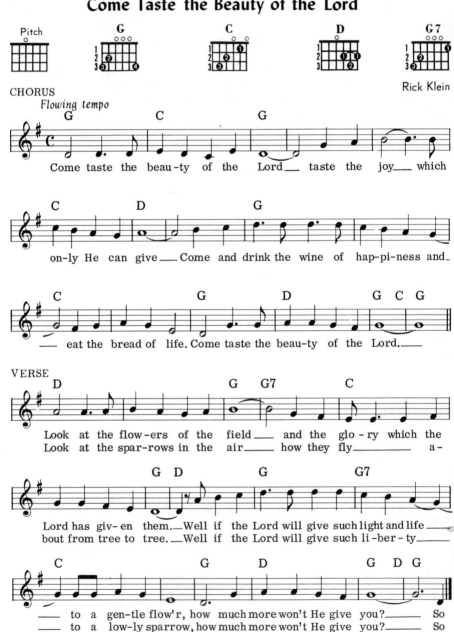

CHORUS

Flowing tempo

Come taste the beau-ty of the Lord__ taste the joy__ which on-ly He can give__ Come and drink the wine of hap-pi-ness and__ eat the bread of life. Come taste the beau-ty of the Lord.__

VERSE

Look at the flow-ers of the field__ and the glo-ry which the Lord has giv-en them.__ Well if the Lord will give such light and life__ to a gen-tle flow'r, how much more won't He give you?__ So

Look at the spar-rows in the air__ how they fly__ a-bout from tree to tree.__ Well if the Lord will give such li-ber-ty__ to a low-ly sparrow, how much more won't He give you?__ So

Oh, How I Love Jesus

By Isacc Watts

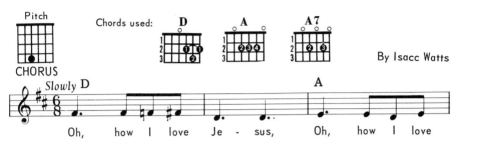

CHORUS

Slowly

Oh, how I love Je - sus, Oh, how I love

Je - sus, ____ Oh, how I love Je - sus, Be -

cause He first loved me. ____ To me He is so

won-der-ful, ____ To me He is so won - der - ful, To

me He is so won-der-ful, ____ Be - cause He first loved me. ____

12

Only Believe

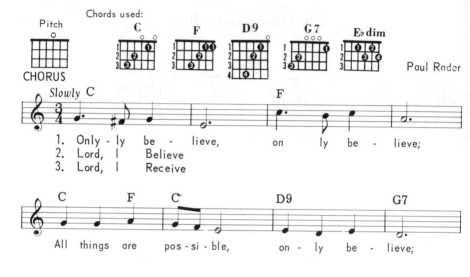

Paul Rader

CHORUS

Slowly

1. Only - ly be - lieve, on - ly be - lieve;
2. Lord, I Believe
3. Lord, I Receive

All things are pos - si - ble, on - ly be - lieve;

On - ly be - lieve, on - ly be - lieve;

All things are pos - si - ble, on - ly be - lieve.

Heavenly Father, We Appreciate You

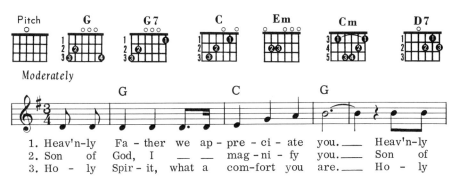

1. Heav'n-ly Fa - ther we ap - pre - ci - ate you. Heav'n-ly
2. Son of God, I __ __ mag - ni - fy you. Son of
3. Ho - ly Spir - it, what a com-fort you are. Ho - ly

Fa - ther, we ap - pre - ci - ate you. We
God __ I __ mag - ni - fy you. You've
Spir - it what a com - fort you are. You

love you, a - dore you __ we bow down be - fore you. Heav'n-ly
cleansed me from sin, and sent the Spir - it with - in. __ Son of
lead us, you guide us; __ you live right in - side us, Ho - ly

Fa - ther, we ap - pre - ci - ate__ you.
God, __ I __ mag - ni - fy__ you.
Spir - it, what a com - fort you__ are.

14   Heaven Came Down and Glory Filled My Soul

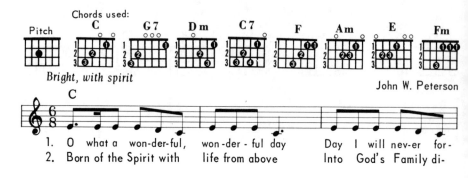

Bright, with spirit

John W. Peterson

1. O what a won-der-ful, won-der-ful day   Day I will nev-er for-
2. Born of the Spirit with life from above   Into God's Family di-

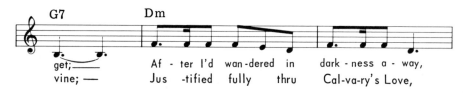

get;___   Af-ter I'd wan-dered in dark-ness a-way,
vine; —   Jus-tified fully thru Cal-va-ry's Love,

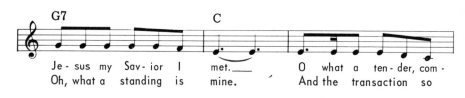

Je-sus my Sav-ior I met.___   O what a ten-der, com-
Oh, what a standing is mine.   And the transaction so

pas-sion-ate Friend   He met the need of my heart;___
quickly was made   when as a sinner I came; —

Shad-ows dis-pel-ing, with joy I am tell-ing, He made all the dark-ness de-
Took of the offer of Grace He did proffer, He save me oh praise His Dear

CHORUS

part!___ Heav - en came down and glo - ry filled my
name. When at the cross the Sav - ior made me

soul, _____ whole; _____

My sins were washed a - way___ And my

night was turned to day___ Heav - en came down and

glo ry filled my soul! _____

C D.C. for verses 2,3

Give Me Oil in My Lamp

(Matthew 25)

A. Sevison

1. Give me some oil in my lamp, keep me burn-ing.___ Give me some oil, in my lamp, I pray___ Give me some oil in my lamp keep me burn-ing.___ keep me burn-ing till the break of day.

CHORUS

Sing Ho-san-nah, Sing Ho-san-nah, Sing Ho-san-nah to the King of kings, Sing Ho-san-nah, Sing Ho-san-nah, Sing Ho-san-nah to the King.___

2. Make me a fisher of men, Keep me seeking, etc...

3. Give me joy in my heart, Keep me singing, etc...

4, Shed your love in my soul, Keep me sharing, etc...

5. Place your peace in my soul, Keep me praising, etc...

6. Place your faith in my heart, Keep me trusting, etc...

7. Hide your word in my heart, Keep me learning, etc...

I've Got Peace Like a River

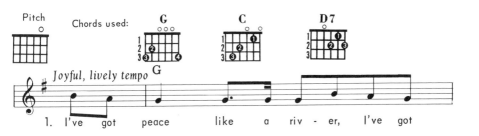

1. I've got peace like a riv-er, I've got peace like a riv-er, I've got peace like a riv-er in my soul; I've got peace like a riv-er, I've got peace like a riv-er, I've got peace like a riv-er in my soul.

2. I've got joy like a fountain, etc...

3. I've got love like an ocean, etc...

18 Taste the Living Water

(John 7:37,38)

Bill Bay

Chords used:

Pitch   A   D   E7   A7

Slowly, with feeling

You can taste the Liv - ing Wa - ter if you come un - to the Lord; All who thirst will find ful - fill - ment In Je - sus Christ the Lord. Pre-cious is the Liv - ing Wa - ter, sweet and gen - tle, Lov - ing peace - ful; Like a riv - er flow - ing smooth - ly From the heart of those who be - lieve. No more hun - ger, thirst, or sor - row shall fall up - on me. I have found my Sav - ior Je - sus, bless-ed liv - ing Trin - i - ty!

With Thy Spirit Fill Me

Pitch — Chords used: D A7 G D7

B. D. Ackley
Oswald J. Smith

1. Lord, pos-sess me now, I pray, Make me whol-ly
2. Lord, I yield my-self to Thee, All I am or
3. Lord, com-mis-sion me, I pray! Souls are dy-ing

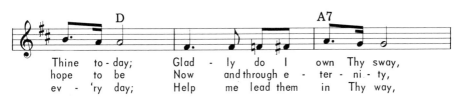

Thine to-day; Glad-ly do I own Thy sway,
hope to be Now and through e-ter-ni-ty,
ev-'ry day; Help me lead them in Thy way,

CHORUS

With Thy Spir-it fill me.
With Thy Spir-it fill me. With Thy Spir-it
With Thy Spir-it fill me.

fill me, With Thy Spir-it fill me;

Make me whol-ly Thine, I pray, With Thy Spir-it fill me.

Turn Your Eyes upon Jesus

Chords used:

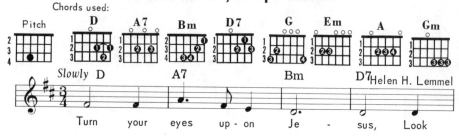

Helen H. Lemmel

Slowly D   A7   Bm   D7

Turn   your   eyes   up-on   Je - sus,   Look

G   Em   A   A7

full   in   His   won-der-ful   face,_____   And the

D   A7   Bm   D7   G   Gm

things   of   earth   will   grow   strange - ly   dim   In the

D   Em   A7   D

light   of   His   glo - ry   and   grace._____

Holy Spirit, Fill Us with His Love

21

Amazing Grace

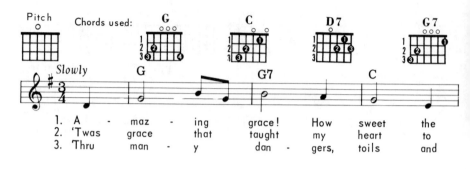

Pitch Chords used: G   C   D7   G7

Slowly

G   G7   C

1. A - maz - ing   grace!   How   sweet   the
2. 'Twas   grace   that   taught   my   heart   to
3. Thru   man - y   dan - gers,   toils   and

G   D7

sound,   That   saved   a   wretch   like   me! _____
fear,   And   grace   my   fears   re - lieved; _____
snares,   I   have   al - read - y   come; _____

D7   G   G7   C

_____   I   once ___ was   lost,   but   now ___ am
_____   How   pre - cious   did   that   grace ___ ap -
_____   'Tis   grace ___ hath   brought   me   safe ___ thus

G   D7   G

found,   Was   blind,   but   now   I   see. _____
pear,   The   hour   I   first   be - lieved! _____
far,   And   grace   will   lead   me   home. _____

4.   When we've been there ten thousand years,
     Bright shining as the sun,
     We've no less days to sing God's praise
     Than when we first begun.

5.   Alleluia, Alleluia, Alleluia, Praise God! (Repeat)

I Will Sing of the Mercies of the Lord

(Psalm 89:1)

J. H. Filmore

To God Be the Glory

Fanny J. Crosby
William H, Doane

1. To God be the glo - ry, great things He hath
2. O per - fect re - demp - tion, the pur - chase of
3. Great things He hath taught us, great things He hath

done; So loved He the world that He gave us His
blood, To ev - 'ry be - liev - er the prom - ise of
done, And great our re - joic - ing through Je - sus the

Son, Who yield - ed His life an a - tone-ment for
God; The vil - est of - fend - er who tru - ly be -
Son; But pur - er, and high - er, and great - er will

sin, And o - pened the life - gate that all may go in.
lieves, That mo - ment from Je - sus a par - don re - ceives.
be Our won - der, our trans-port, when Je - sus we see.

REFRAIN

Praise the Lord, praise the Lord, Let the earth hear His voice! Praise the

Lord, praise the Lord, Let the peo-ple re - joice! O come to the Fa-ther, thro'

Je - sus the Son, And give Him the glo - ry, great things He hath done.

I Lift Up My Hands in Thy Name
25

based on Matthew 11:28-30
and Psalm 63   ('Travis' or country finger-style guitar
accompaniment recommended)

Hallelujah!

(Psalm 150)

Hal-le lu, hal-le-lu, hal-le-lu, hal-le-lu-jah! Praise ye the Lord! Hal-le-

lu, hal-le-lu, hal-le-lu, hal-le-lu-jah! Praise ye the Lord!

Praise ye the Lord, hal-le-lu-jah! Praise ye the Lord, hal-le-lu-jah!

Praise ye the Lord, hal-le-lu-jah! Praise ye the Lord!

Praise Him in the Morning

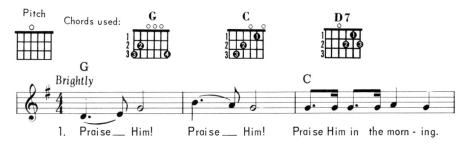

1. Praise__ Him! Praise __ Him! Praise Him in the morn - ing.

Praise Him in the noon - time. Praise__ Him! Praise__ Him!

Praise Him when the sun goes down.

2. Love Him ...

3. Trust Him ...

4. Serve Him ...

5. Jesus ...

Jesus, Lord!

28

I See the Lord!

(Isaiah 6:1-3)

There Is Power In the Blood

All We Need is Jesus

('Travis' or country finger-style guitar
accompaniment recommended)

Bill Bay

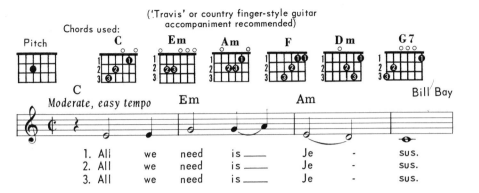

1. All we need is —— Je - sus.
2. All we need is —— Je - sus.
3. All we need is —— Je - sus.

Fill us with your —— love.
Grant us u - ni - ty.
Guide us through each —— day.

Dwell with - in our —— hearts ——
King - dom, Pow'r and the glo - ry.
Fill us with your —— Spir - it.

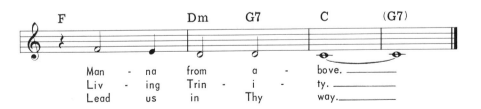

Man - na from a - bove. ——
Liv - ing Trin - i - ty. ——
Lead us in Thy way.——

Surely Goodness and Mercy

John W. Peterson
Alfred B. Smith

1. A pil - grim was I, and a - wan - d'ring, In the cold night of sin I did roam, When Je - sus, the kind Shep - herd found me, And now I am on my way home.

CHORUS

Sure - ly good - ness and mer - cy shall fol - low me All the days, all the days of my life; Sure - ly good - ness and mer - cy shall fol - low

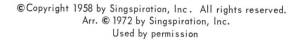

me All the days, all the days of my life. ____

And I shall dwell in the house of the Lord for -

ev - er, And I shall feast at the ta - ble spread for me; ____

____ Sure - ly good - ness and mer - cy shall fol - low

me All the days, all the days of my life, ____

____ All the days, all the days of my life. ____

2. He restoreth my soul when I'm weary,
   He giveth me strength day by day;
   He leads me beside the still waters,
   He guards me each step of the way. (Chorus)

3. When I walk thru the dark lonesome valley,
   My Savior will walk with me there;
   And safely His great hand will lead me
   To the mansions He's gone to prepare. (Chorus)

Holy Spirit, Dwell In Me

1. There have been names that I have loved to hear, But
2. There is no name in earth or heav'n a - bove, That
3. And some day I shall see Him face to face To

nev - er has there been a name so dear To this heart of mine,
we should give such hon-or and such love, As the bless-ed name,
thank and praise him for His won-drous grace, Which He gave to me,

as the name di-vine, The pre-cious, pre-cious name of Je - sus.
let us all ac-claim, That won-drous, glo-rious name of Je - sus.
when He made me free, The bless-ed Son of God called Je - sus.

CHORUS

Je - sus is the sweet-est name I know, And He's

just the same as His love-ly name, And that's the rea-son why I love Him

so; Oh; Je-sus is the sweet-est name I know.

I Know Where I'm Goin'

(Finger-style guitar accompaniment)

Ray Dahrouge and Mickey Holiday

Moderate, easy feeling

1. One day I was won-d'ring, What's it all a - bout?
2. There are man - y man - sions He's pre-par - ing there
3. Friend, if you are search - ing for a bet - ter way, I'm

Life is full of heart - break, rest - less-ness and doubt;
That could not be pur - chased by a mil - lion - aire;
Rec - om - mend - ing Je - sus trust in Him to - day,

Then a gen - tle stran - ger whis-pered words of love,
Streets of gold that glit - ter, gates of pearl - y white.
He will give life mean - ing like no oth - er can,

Point - ed me to heav - en, wrote my name a - bove.
In a day e - ter - nal where there is no night.
Come and trav - el with me to the prom - ised land.

CHORUS

{ I know where I'm go - in'____ and who I'm gon - na
{ He has giv - en some - thing__ that on - ly He could

see I have a friend named Je - sus
give He gave His life in pay - ment

1. wait - ing there for me!
2. so that I could live.____

Kum Ba Yah

(Come by Here)

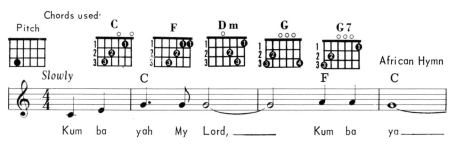

African Hymn

Kum ba yah My Lord, _____ Kum ba ya _____

_____ Kum ba ya My Lord, _____ Kum ba Yah _____

_____ Kum ba yah My Lord _____ Kum ba yah _____

_____ Oh Lord, _____ Kum ba yah. _____

2. Someone's crying Lord, Kum ba yah (3 times)
   Oh Lord, Kum ba yah.

3. Someone's praying Lord, Kum ba yah (3 times)
   Oh Lord, Kum ba yah.

4. Someone's singing Lord, Kum ba Yah (3 times)
   Oh Lord, Kum ba yah.

38 Behold What Manner of Love!

(1 *John* 3)

* Guitar - Capo 1st Fret And Play Following Chords

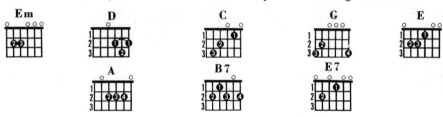

NANCY THOMPSON SEBASTIAN

CHORUS

Gently
(Descant opt)

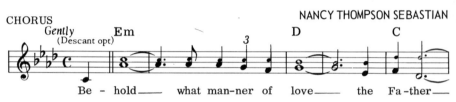

Be - hold___ what man-ner of love___ the Fa-ther___

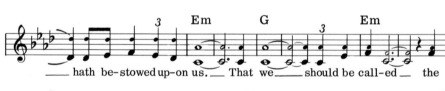

___ hath be-stowed up-on us.___ That we___ should be call-ed___ the

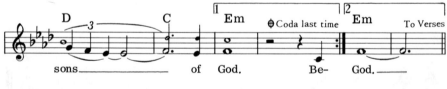

sons_____ of God.   Be-   God.___

VERSE

1. Be - lov-ed now__ are we the sons__ of God____ and it
2. And ev-'ry man__ that has this hope__ in Him____
3. Who - ev-er shall__con-fess Je-sus__is Lord____

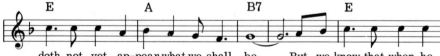

doth not yet ap-pear what we shall   be.___ But we know that when he
pur - i - fies him-self as Christ is   pure.___ And ye know that he was
God dwell-eth in him and he in   God.___ And we know and have be-

Let Us Break Bread Together

40

1. Let us break bread to-geth-er on our knees, _____ (on our knees) Let us break bread to-geth-er on our knees _____ (on our knees) When I fall on my knees with my face to the ris - ing sun, O ___ Lord, have mer-cy on me! _____

2. Let us drink wine (or the cup) together on our knees, etc...

3. Let us bow 'round the altar on our knees, etc...

4. Let us praise God together on our knees, etc...

Walk in the Spirit

(Galatians 5:25)

41

Bill Bay

1. Hum - bly we seek____ to serve Christ Je - sus
2. We are u - ni - ted in prais - ing Je - sus
3. Walk in the Spir - it yield - ing dai - ly

and we for - give ev - 'ry - one.____
one in the
to His pure

Spir - it of God____ we pray.____ What a

Ho - li - ness in____ our hearts.____

CHORUS

Joy and a priv - 'ledge to trust and o - bey____ and

tell of His won - der - ful love.____

Jesus Breaks Every Fetter

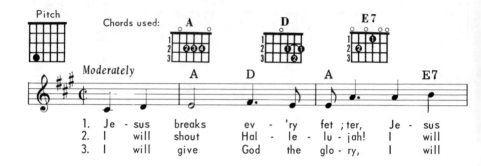

1. Je - sus breaks ev - 'ry fet ; ter, Je - sus
2. I will shout Hal - le - lu - jah! I will
3. I will give God the glo - ry, I will

breaks ev - 'ry fet - ter, Je - sus breaks ev - 'ry
shout Hal - le - lu - jah! I will shout Hal - le -
give God the glo - ry, I will give God the

fet - ter, And He sets me free.
lu - jah! For He sets me free.
glo - ry, For He sets me free.

Take My Life and Let It Be

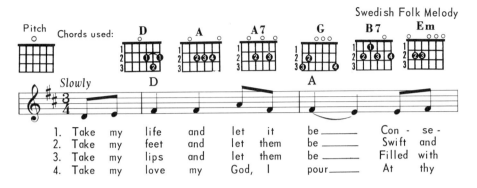

Peace I Give You

Bill Bay

1. "Peace, peace I give you,
2. Come un - to Je - sus,
3. Je - sus is liv - ing,
4. We sing our praise to

Not like that you have known.
All whose souls search for rest.
In our hearts He a - bides.
God and Je - sus His Son.

Peace, peace I leave you,"
His yoke is eas - y,
God's grace in Je - sus,
And with God's Spir - it,

Je - sus re - ceives you as His own.
Seek Him and sure ly you'll be blessed.
Sav - ing and fill - ing emp - ty lives.
Our vic - to - ry has been won.

Gethsemane, Destiny!

45

Do, Lord

46

Spiritual

1. I've got a home in glo-ry-land that out-shines the sun,
2. I took Je-sus as my Sav-ior, you take Him too,

I've got a home in glo-ry-land that out-shines the sun,
I took Je-sus as my Sav-ior, you take Him too,

(O Lordy!)

I've got a home in glo-ry-land that out-shines the sun ___
I took ___ Je-sus as my Sav-ior, you take Him too, ___

(Hallelujah!)

'way be-yond ___ the blue.
while He's cal-ling you.

Do, Lord O do, Lord, O do re-mem-ber me, Do, Lord O do, Lord O

(O Lordy)

do re-mem-ber me, Do, Lord O do, Lord, O

(Hallelujah)

do re-mem-ber me ___ 'way be-yond the blue.

Oh, Sinner Man

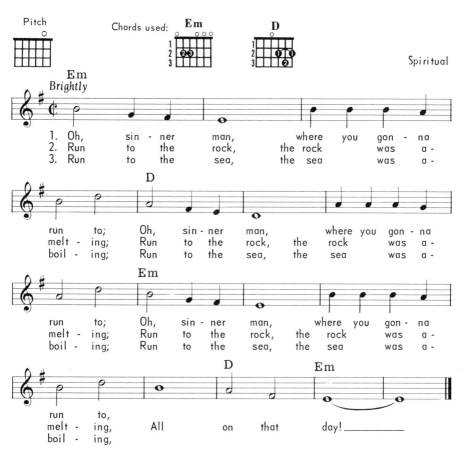

Pitch

Chords used: **Em**   **D**

Spiritual

Em
Brightly

1. Oh, sin - ner man, where you gon - na
2. Run to the rock, the rock was a -
3. Run to the sea, the sea was a -

D

run to; Oh, sin - ner man, where you gon - na
melt - ing; Run to the rock, the rock was a -
boil - ing; Run to the sea, the sea was a -

Em

run to; Oh, sin - ner man, where you gon - na
melt - ing; Run to the rock, the rock was a -
boil - ing; Run to the sea, the sea was a -

D   **Em**

run to,
melt - ing, All on that day! _____
boil - ing,

4. Run to the moon, the moon was a-bleeding, (3 times)
   All on that day.

5. Run to the Lord, Lord won't you hide me? (3 times)
   All on that day.

6. Run to the Devil, Devil was a-waiting; (3 times)
   All on that day.

7. Oh, sinner man, you oughta been a-praying, (3 times)
   All on that day.

8. Oh, sinner man, you should have found Jesus; (3 times)
   Long before that day.

Feed My Lambs

Charles A, Buffham

4. Peter heard the cock when it crew;
   As he left he wept, and he knew!
   Everyone of us is guilty too;
   That's why Jesus died - just for you!

5. Repeat verse one

Signs Shall Follow

49

Michael Row the Boat Ashore

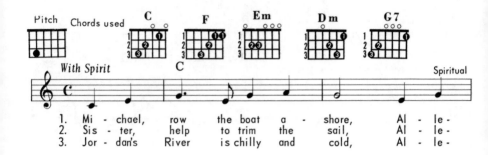

1. Mi - chael, row the boat a - shore, Al - le -
2. Sis - ter, help to trim the sail, Al - le -
3. Jor - dan's River is chilly and cold, Al - le -

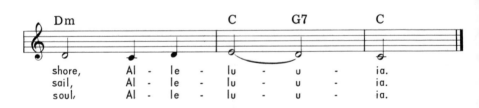

lu - ia, Mi - chael, row the boat a -
lu - ia, Sis - ter, help to trim the
lu - ia, Chills the body but not the

shore, Al - le - lu - u - ia.
sail, Al - le - lu - u - ia.
soul, Al - le - lu - u - ia.

4. Jordan's River is deep and wide,
   Hallelujah!
   Milk and honey on the other side,
   Hallelujah!

5. I have heard the good news too,
   Hallelujah!
   I have heard the good news too,
   Hallelujah!

6. Repeat verse one

In the Spirit of God

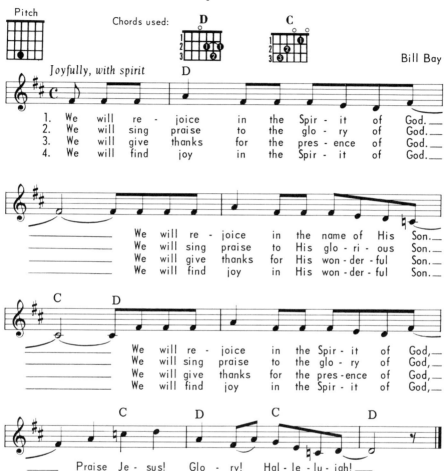

Bill Bay

Joyfully, with spirit

1. We will re - joice in the Spir - it of God. __
2. We will sing praise to the glo - ry of God. __
3. We will give thanks for the pres - ence of God. __
4. We will find joy in the Spir - it of God. __

We will re - joice in the name of His Son. __
We will sing praise to His glo - ri - ous Son. __
We will give thanks for His won - der - ful Son. __
We will find joy in His won - der - ful Son. __

We will re - joice in the Spir - it of God, __
We will sing praise to the glo - ry of God, __
We will give thanks for the pres - ence of God, __
We will find joy in the Spir - it of God, __

Praise Je - sus! Glo - ry! Hal - le - lu - jah! __

5. We will find peace in the Spirit of God,
We will find peace in His wonderful Son.
We will find peace in the Spirit of God,
Praise Jesus! Glory! Hallelujah!

6. We will find love in the Spirit of God.
We will find love in His wonderful Son.
We will find love in the Spirit of God,
Praise Jesus! Glory! Hallelujah!

7. We're gonna trust in the Spirit of God.
We're gonna trust in His wonderful Son.
We're gonna trust in the Spirit of God,
Praise Jesus! Glory! Hallelujah!

8. We are one in the Spirit of God.
We are one with His wonderful Son.
We are one in the Spirit of God,
Praise Jesus! Glory! Hallelujah!

52

Oh, What a Day That Will Be

Bill Bay

1. Soon we're gon-na see Lord Je-sus, Soon we're gon-na see Lord Je-sus,
2. Now we see the Spir-it flow-ing, Now we see the Spir-it flow-ing,

Soon He's gon-na come to take His, bride. Glo - ry!
Now we see the Spir - it flow - ing ev - 'ry - where!

Soon we're gon-na see Lord Je - sus, Soon we're gon-na see Lord Je - sus,
Now we see the Spir - it flow-ing, Now we see the Spir-it flow-ing,

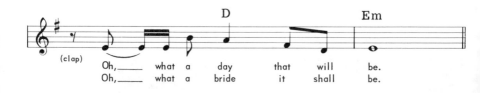

Oh, _____ what a day that will be.
Oh, _____ what a bride it shall be.

CHORUS

Fol - low Je - sus. Serve Lord Je - sus.

Hear His cal - ling now!

(clap) Gath - er-ing the har-vest with Him (clap) Gath - er-ing the har-vest with Him.

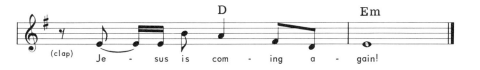

(clap) Je - sus is com - ing a - gain!

54   Shine

Majorie Jones

Chords used:

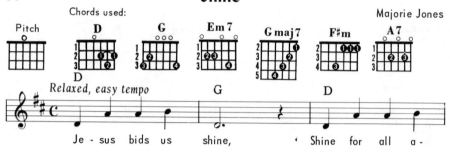

Je - sus bids us shine,   Shine for all a-

round.   Man - y kinds of dark - ness in the

world   are   found,   Sin, and want, and

sor - row;   So   we   must   shine——

You in your small cor - ner, and I in mine.

Lord, I Want to Be a Christian

55

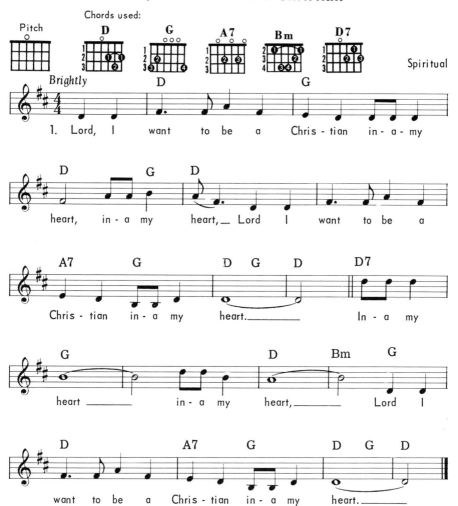

2. Lord, I want to be more loving in-a my heart, etc...

3. Lord, I want to be more holy in-a my heart, etc...

4. Lord, I want to be like Jesus in-a my heart, etc...

God Is so Good

African Christian Folk Song

Chords used:

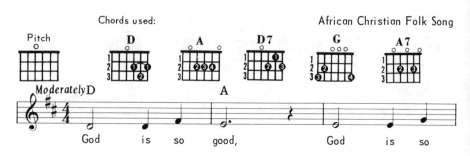

Moderately

God is so good, God is so

good, God is so good, He's so

good to me.

2. God cares for me, etc...

3. God leads me on, etc...

4. I'll do His will, etc...

5. Jesus is Lord, etc...

6. I'll trust in Him, etc...

7. I'll sing His praise, etc...

Fill My Cup, Lord

Richard Blanchard

1. Like the wom-an at the well I was seek-ing ___ For things that could not sat-is - fy. And then I heard my Sav-ior speak-ing:___ "Draw from my well that nev-er shall run dry."

2. There are mil-lions in this world who are crav-ing ___ The pleas-ure earth-ly things af-ford. But none can match the won-drous treas-ure ___ That I find in Je-sus Christ, my Lord.

3. So, my broth-er if the things this world gave you ___ Leave hun-gers that won't pass a-way. My bless-ed Lord will come and save you ___ If you kneel to Him and hum-bly pray:

CHORUS

Fill my cup, Lord,___ I lift it up Lord.___ Come and quench this thirst-ing of my soul. Bread of heav-en, feed me till I want no more, Fill my cup, fill it up and make me whole.

58

Fill Me, Jesus

Ron Salsbury

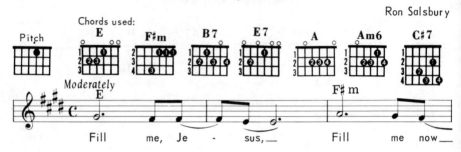

Chords used:

Fill me, Je - sus, — Fill me now —

Fill me, Je - sus — with Thy

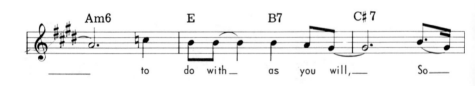

pre - cious ho - ly pow'r. — I am yours, my Lord, —

to do with — as you will, — So —

fill me, Je - sus, — right now.

Springs of Living Water

59

I Will Follow Him

60

Bill Bay

Lyrics:

1. I will fol-low Him where He leads me. With my Lord I'll go, I will fol-low Him, sav-ing souls from sin. I love Him so.

2. I shall tell of Him where He leads me. By God's Spirit they'l know that He died for us and He lives for us, His truth shall grow.

Serv - ing the Lord, Christ Je-sus the King! He is the way, His praise I will sing. The Good Shep-herd leads and strength-ens me, In His name I shall go. Sav-ior Je-sus, Lamb of God. I love you so.

We'll Give the Glory to Jesus

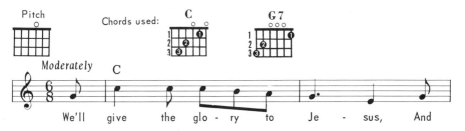

We'll give the glo - ry to Je - sus, And tell of His love, and tell of His love; We'll give the glo - ry to Je - sus, And tell of His won - der - ful Love.

I Love Him Better Every Day

S. E. Cox

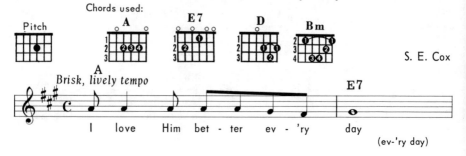

Chords used:

Brisk, lively tempo

I love Him bet - ter ev - 'ry day

(ev-'ry day)

I love Him bet - ter ev - 'ry day;

(ev-'ry day)

Close by His side I will a - bide,

I love Him bet - ter ev - 'ry day.

2. I'll serve Him better every day, etc...

3. I'll praise His glory every day, etc...

4. I'll worship Jesus every day, etc...

Isn't He Wonderful

Chords used:

S. Jones

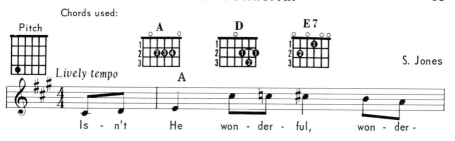

Is - n't He won - der - ful, won - der -

ful, won - der - ful, Is - n't Je - sus, my Lord won - der -

ful! Eyes have seen, ears have heard, It's re -

cord - ed in God's Word, Is - n't Je - sus, my Lord won - der - ful!

64

And I Believe Him

Dennis Gilbert

Moderately, with feeling

1. I heard a young man ___ died for free - dom. ___
2. I met a young man ___ in a val - ley.
3. I've grown to feel that ___ young man's pres - ence, ___

___ I heard a young man ___ died for
___ I met a young man ___ in my
___ I've grown to know the ___ rea - sons

ev - 'ry - one. ___ They tell me He
heart one day. ___ He told me that
why ___ He tells me I

nev - er ___ sold His con - science. ___
I would ___ nev - er lose Him. ___
have so ___ much to live for. ___ He

They tell me He nev - er ___ sold His love. ___
He told me that He will ___ al - ways love me. ___
prom - is - es much more than ___ I can ask for. ___

___ And I be - lieve them! ___
___ And I be - lieve Him! ___
___ And I be - lieve Him! ___

I Was In His Mind

65

Finger-style guitar

Jane LaRowe

Slowly

1. I was in His mind__ be-fore the worlds were made,__ I was
2. I was in His thoughts__ the night He prayed for me,____ I was

D.C. I am in His mind,___ and soon He'll come for me,____ I am

in His mind__ be-fore earth's frame was__ laid,__ Be-cause He
in His thoughts__ be-fore Geth-se-ma-ne,____ Be-cause He
in His mind___ with Him in heav'n to__ be,____ Be-cause He

knew me,_____ be-cause He loved me!
saw me,_____ be-cause He loved me!____
wants me,_____ be-cause He

Boldly

I was in His heart____ when Cal-v'ry's hill He climbed,

____ I was in His heart____ when He died for all man-kind,

____ Be-cause He sought me, be-cause He loved me!____

[3]

ritard

loves me,____ be-cause He loves____ me!____

66

The Victory Is Found In Jesus

Bill Bay

© Copyright 1972 by Mel Bay Publications, Inc. Kirkwood, Missouri.
All rights reserved

Victory In Jesus

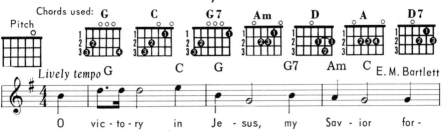

E. M. Bartlett

O vic - to - ry in Je - sus, my Sav - ior for -

ev - er, He sought me and bought me with

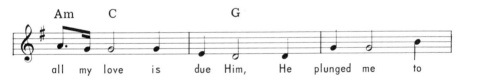

His re - deem - ing blood; He loved me ere I knew Him, and

all my love is due Him, He plunged me to

vic - to - ry be - neath the cleans - ing flood.

Give Unto the Lord
(From Psalm 29)

Rick Klein

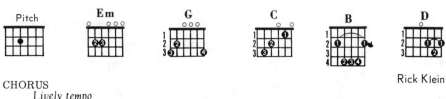

CHORUS
Lively tempo

Give un-to the Lord_ O ye might-y na-tions; give un-to the Lord_

glo - ry and strength. Give un-to the Lord,_O ye might - y na-tions; _

give un -to the Lord all the glo -ry due his name. _____ 1. The
4. The

1st and 4th
VERSE

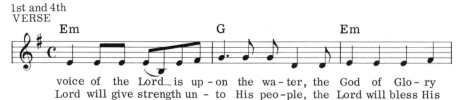

voice of the Lord_is up - on the wa - ter, the God of Glo - ry
Lord will give strength un - to His peo-ple, the Lord will bless His

thun-der-eth. The Lord of_____ Lords is up - on man-y wa-ters, so
peo-ple with peace. The Lord will give strength un - to His_ peo-ple, so

give un -to the Lord all the glo - ry due His name._____ Oh__
give un -to the Lord all the glo - ry due His name._____ Oh__

2nd and 3rd
VERSE

2. Voice of the Lord is pow-er-ful, the voice of the Lord is full, the
3. Voice of the Lord di - vid-eth the__ Flames _____ of fire, the

voice of the Lord is full of maj - es - ty. The voice of the Lord is
voice of the Lord shak-eth the wil -der-ness. The voice of the Lord di-

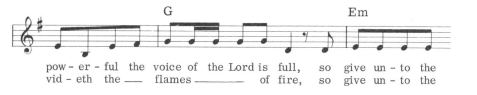

pow - er-ful the voice of the Lord is full, so give un - to the
vid - eth the __ flames _____ of fire, so give un - to the

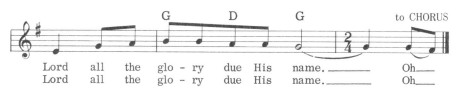

Lord all the glo - ry due His name. _____ Oh__
Lord all the glo - ry due His name. _____ Oh__

The Greatest Gift

Phil Perkins

Moderately

1. My hands I give_____ to use for Thee,_____
2. My heart I pledge_____ to love for Thee,_____
3. My life I give_____ to live for Thee,_____

_____ For yours are torn_____ from Cal - va - ry._____
_____ For yours did break_____ on Cal - va - ry._____
_____ For yours you gave_____ on Cal - va - ry._____

_____ Those hands that knew_____ a car - pen - ter's
_____ A heart that knew_____ no love _____ in
_____ A life God sent_____ to set _____ us

trade_____ were nailed that day_____ for me to
death._____ My heart I give_____ its love to
free. _____ Here, Lord, I give _____ my life to

shed. ____ No great-er gift ____ can ev - er
save. ____
Thee. ____

be ____ than that which God ____ did give to

me. ____ For long a - go ____ He gave to

us ____ the great-est gift ____ we'll e'er re - ceive. ____

Jacob's Ladder

Chords used:

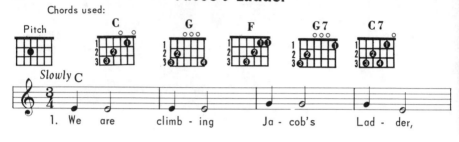

Slowly C

1. We are climb - ing Ja - cob's Lad - der,

We are climb - ing Ja - cob's Lad - der,

We are climb - ing Ja - cob's Lad - der,

Sol - diers of the Cross.

2. Every round goes higher, higher,   (3 times)
   Soldier of the cross.

3. Sinner, do you love my Jesus?   (3 times)
   Soldier of the cross.

4. If you love Him, why not serve him?   (3 times)
   Soldier of the cross.

5. We are climbing higher, higher,   (3 times)
   Soldier of the cross.

6. Rise, Shine, give God glory,   (3 times)
   Soldier of the cross.

His Sheep Am I

Orien Johnson

In God's green pas-tures feed-ing; by His cool wa-ters lie
Soft in the ev -'ning walk my Lord and I; All the
sheep of His pas-ture fare so won-drous-ly fine

His sheep am I. Wa-ters cool, Pas-tures
Dark the night, rough the
(In the valley,)
(In the valley,)

green, In the ev -'ning walk my Lord and I;
way Step by step, —— my Lord and
(on the mountain) (In the ev -'ning walk my Lord and I;)
(on the mountain) (Step by step my Lord and

I.
I.)

74 Seasons of Rapture

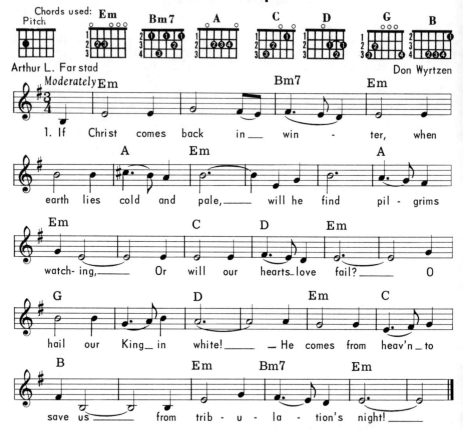

Arthur L. Farstad

Don Wyrtzen

Moderately

1. If Christ comes back in __ win - ter, when earth lies cold and pale, __ will he find pil - grims watch- ing, __ Or will our hearts love fail? __ O hail our King __ in white! __ — He comes from heav'n __ to save us __ from trib - u - la - tion's night!

2. If Christ comes back in springtime,
When burst the buds leaf-green,
He will gather up His garlands,
God's saints, from earth's dark scene.
O hail our Bride-groom King!
He comes His Bride to rapture:
How can we help but sing?

3. If Christ comes back in summer,
When shines the orange sun,
Will He find Christians toiling
In love, with hearts as one?
O hail our great Sun-King,
With healing splendor rising
To draw us to His wing.

4. If Christ comes back in autumn,
When grow the fields with gold,
He will reap with joy His wheat sheaves
Which He did plant of old.
O hail! our Lord shall come
To gather in His loved ones
And shout His "Harvest Home!"

Have Thine Own Way, Lord

Ten Camels Bearing Gifts

(Genesis 24)

Bill Bay

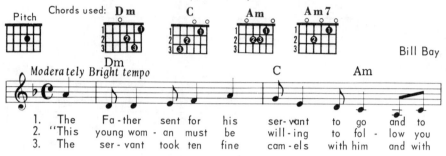

1. The Fa-ther sent for his ser-vant to go and to
2. "This young wom-an must be will-ing to fol-low you
3. The ser-vant took ten fine cam-els with him and with

find a bride for his son; The ser-vant said, "I will
out of her na-tive land; For I will not send my
gifts they be-gan their ride; The wealth of his mas-ter

seek and I'll search 'till I find God's — cho-sen — one.
son there a-gain e-ven to join his bride hand in hand."
was in his care for to give to the cho-sen — bride.

Ease your mind, Seek and find.
Fol-low him, Go with him.
Fol-low him, Go with him.

4. He journeyed all day and came to a well and he said, "It shall surely be,
   The daughter who gives me water to drink shall be chosen to go with me."
   Receive Him, Serve Him.

5. Rebekah came to the well that night and the servant ran out to her.
   She met him and gave him water to drink, just as he said it would occur.
   Receive Him, Serve Him.

6. The servant went to her family and said, "She is chosen to be his bride."
   They said, "It proceedeth from the Lord, In God's will we shall abide."
   Go to Him, Be with Him.

7. Rebekah received the silver and gold and fine raiment was given too;
   She said, "Though I have not seen this young man, I will certainly follow you."
   Go to Him, Be with Him.

8. Rebekah arose and followed the man, thus the servant led her his way.
   And soon she looked up and saw the son, what a glorious sight that day.
   Come to Him, Dwell with Him.

9. The son took Rebekah to be his wife and they lived in his father's land.
   The father gave all his blessings to them and forever they walked hand in hand.
   Come to Him, Dwell with Him.

10. This story took place a long time ago and it will come to pass again.
    The Spirit will find God's chosen Bride to be with Jesus Christ in the end.
    Praise Him, worship Him.

All Hail the Power of Jesus' Name

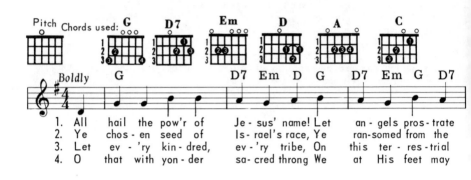

Pitch — Chords used: G   D7   Em   D   A   C

Boldly

G ... D7 Em D G D7 Em G D7

1. All hail the pow'r of Je-sus' name! Let an-gels pros-trate
2. Ye chos-en seed of Is-rael's race, Ye ran-somed from the
3. Let ev-'ry kin-dred, ev-'ry tribe, On this ter-res-trial
4. O that with yon-der sa-cred throng We at His feet may

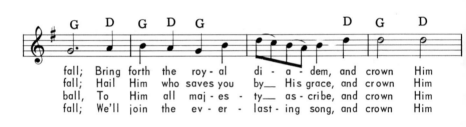

G D G D G   D G D

fall; Bring forth the roy-al di-a-dem, and crown Him
fall; Hail Him who saves you by— His grace, and crown Him
ball, To Him all maj-es-ty— as-cribe, and crown Him
fall; We'll join the ev-er- last-ing song, and crown Him

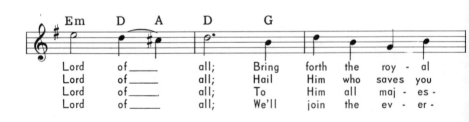

Em D A D G

Lord of____ all; Bring forth the roy-al
Lord of____ all; Hail Him who saves you
Lord of____ all; To Him all maj-es-
Lord of____ all; We'll join the ev-er-

D7 Em G C G D7 G

di-a-dem, And crown Him Lord____ of all.
by— His grace, And crown Him Lord____ of all.
ty— as-cribe, And crown Him Lord____ of all.
last-ing song, And crown Him Lord____ of all.

Oh Come, Let Us Adore Him

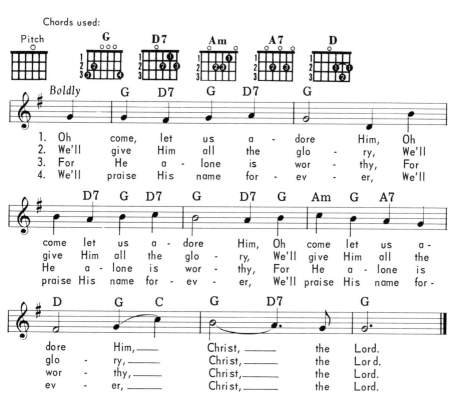

Chords used:

1. Oh come, let us a - dore Him, Oh
2. We'll give Him all the glo - ry, We'll
3. For He a - lone is wor - thy, For
4. We'll praise His name for - ev - er, We'll

come let us a - dore Him, Oh come let us a -
give Him all the glo - ry, We'll give Him all the
He a - lone is wor - thy, For He a - lone is
praise His name for - ev - er, We'll praise His name for -

dore Him, _____ Christ, _____ the Lord.
glo - ry, _____ Christ, _____ the Lord.
wor - thy, _____ Christ, _____ the Lord.
ev - er, _____ Christ, _____ the Lord.

Jesus, Everywhere

Bill Bay

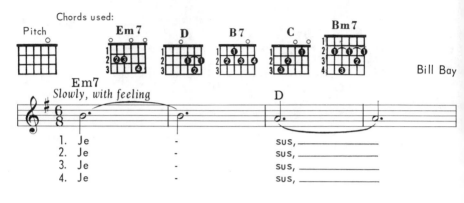

Chords used:

Pitch | Em7 | D | B7 | C | Bm7

Slowly, with feeling

1. Je - sus, _____
2. Je - sus, _____
3. Je - sus, _____
4. Je - sus, _____

hear _____ our call. _____
hear _____ our prayer. _____
if _____ peo-ple knew. _____
we _____ give you praise. _____

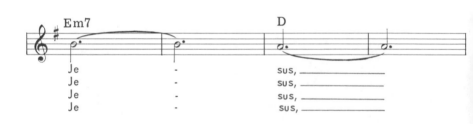

Je - sus, _____
Je - sus, _____
Je - sus, _____
Je - sus, _____

Grant u - ni - ty to us all. _____
pour forth God's Spirit ev - 'ry - where. _____
Heav - en on earth lies in You. _____
Teach us to fol - low Thy way. _____